DOGMAN

FRIGHTENING ENCOUNTERS

Volume 2

Compiled and edited by
Tom Lyons

DOGMAN FRIGHTENING ENCOUNTERS: VOLUME 2

Copyright © 2019 Tom Lyons

All rights reserved. No part of this may be reproduced in any form or by any means without the prior consent of the author, except brief quotes used in reviews.

All information and opinions expressed in *Dogman Frightening Encounters: Volume 2* are based upon personal perspectives and experiences of those who were generous enough to submit them. Tom Lyons does not purport the information presented in this book is based on accurate, current, or valid scientific knowledge.

Acknowledgments

It's certainly no easy task for people to discuss their encounters with the strange species. I'd like to personally thank the many good people out there who took the time and energy to put their experiences into writing.

Out of respect for those who were involved, a few of the names have been altered or replaced with "anonymous".

Would you like to see your report in an issue of *"Dogman Frightening Encounters"*?

If so, all you need to do is type up a summary of your experience, and email it to Tom Lyons at:

Living.Among.Bigfoot@gmail.com

Special Offer

If you submit a report and it is accepted, you will receive an exclusive paperback copy signed by Tom, shortly after the book is released. If you'd like to participate in that offer, be sure to include your mailing address in the email.

Contents

Report #1 1

Report #2 10

Report #3 18

Report #4 37

Report #5 51

Report #6 66

Report #7 75

Report #8 83

Editor's Note 95

Mailing List Sign Up Form 97

Social Media 99

About the Editor 101

Report #1

Hello, y'all, my name is Kitty, and when I was the age of 20, I encountered what I believe to be either a dogman or a skin-walker. No, I didn't see a human transform into the creature, but I almost find it harder to believe that this organism that walks around on two legs is a creation of Mother Nature.

My hair-raising experience happened in a small Texas town known as Marfa. I lived there for the first 22 years of my life, and man, am I happy I saved up enough money to get out of there. The place is so depressing and never has anything going on. It's why so many people there are alcoholics and drug addicts. If I hadn't gotten out of there when I did, I might've headed down that dangerous route.

If any of you have ever been to Marfa, you know that it looks more like a place where you would run into aliens, or extraterrestrials, or whatever. That almost made seeing this two-legged canine even more surprising. I was with my ex-boyfriend, and we were sitting in his car, listening to tunes while he smoked a cigarette. That guy used to chain smoke like a madman. He probably still does. Actually, he's probably dead. He always had the same posture, where he would hang his left arm outside his rolled-down window and would turn his head to blow the smoke outside. He took pride in thinking his car smelled brand-new, but the funny thing is, it stank so bad! If it weren't for his devastating good looks and charisma, I wouldn't have even gone on a single date with that man.

So, we were sitting in his car for like the 100th time, watching the sunset over this vast desert land, when suddenly I saw something very odd out of my peripheral vision. As I turned to see what it was, I saw what I first thought was a man running toward the driver's side window. But it was running in such a weird way, and it looked to have the head of a coyote; at least, that's the best description I can give it. Whatever it was, it didn't look at all friendly, and I had to shake my ex-boyfriend's arm to get his attention and have him roll up the window. The creature was pretty quiet on its way to the car, and I'm not so certain that my ex would have kept his left arm if it wasn't for me frantically notifying him of what was headed toward us.

As soon as the window rolled up, my ex slammed his palm on the car horn, which caused the creature to halt once it got within about five feet from us. It was clear that it hated that noise since it started scratching at its large ears. That's when I noticed that it had hands, not paws like a normal dog. I could see thumbs. Eventually, my ex became so distracted by the sight of this thing, that his hand naturally slipped off the car horn.

We then watched as the creature walked a few laps around the vehicle. This happened way back in the day before cellphones with cameras were available to everyone.

Since we were there for the sunset, it was getting darker by the second while we watched this creature that was unlike anything either of us had ever seen before, even on TV. I mean, it was so shocking, that neither of us even thought to shift the car into drive and scram. It truly was as if the creature had us entranced. I'm sure that if there had been a hidden camera recording us, we'd be wide-eyed with our mouths hanging open. It wasn't long before I started coughing, failing to realize that the interior of the car had filled up with smoke from the still-lit cigarette. Out of nowhere, the creature ran to a position that was about 20 or 30 yards away from the hood of the car. It then turned around and ran toward us on two legs before leaping onto the hood. The creature was so heavy that its weight caused the rear tires to lift off the ground briefly. At least, that's how it felt if you were sitting inside of it. As the creature pressed its snout against the windshield, that's when my ex finally got the idea to shift the car in reverse.

The creature was so agile, and it effortlessly hopped off the hood of the vehicle as soon as we started moving. I watched as it then growled at us while we spun the car around and headed toward the main road. I was expecting the creature to chase us until we got going at a very high speed, but it didn't; it just stood there watching us disappear into the horizon. Aside from the terror of the event, something that always stood out to me was how my ex quit smoking cigarettes after it happened. It was as if the guy had stared death right in the face and then started valuing his life more.

You may or may not be surprised to hear that we didn't discuss the incident too much after it happened. However, we weren't together for too much longer after it happened, so maybe we didn't have enough time to accept the bizarre reality before we felt like trying to put it into words. Our relationship was already on the rocks beforehand. I've told a few other close friends, boyfriends, girlfriends, about it, but I never feel like anyone truly believes me. I mean, it is a pretty weird thing to bring up.

I get what Tom Lyons is saying when, once you see something like this, it alters your perspective on the world. I found that there is a period where you distrust all authority, as well as modern-day science. It feels as though you've been lied to and that you need to relearn the truth about this existence. Everything you were taught in school flies out the window. But, at the same time, I found the feeling to be liberating. It affirms that you're not at all crazy for ever having considered any "conspiracy theories".

It might surprise many, but I've spent quite a bit of time out in nature since that event, and never again saw anything like that. And that's a good thing! There are so many people that go searching for these kinds of creatures, and that's something I'll never be able to relate to. Why would you want to look for something that could so easily kill and eat you?

-Submitted by Kitty K.

Report #2

Year: 2000

Location: Minocqua, Wisconsin

My name is Jonathan, and I had an encounter with what I believe was a dogman when I was 12 years old and on a summer vacation with my family. I grew up in the Milwaukee area, and it was a tradition for us for a long time to go up to Minocqua for about a week every summer. If you're not familiar with Minocqua, it is a pleasant and quiet lake town in the northern part of the state. My little brother was ten years younger than me, so at the time, he couldn't participate in a whole lot. He would usually stay at the resort and do stuff with my mom while my dad and I would go fishing. I can't remember what the river was called because it's been so long since I've been there, but the locals knew it to have plenty of fish. Dad and I always had good luck when we'd cast out into that river. Usually, we would catch enough panfish to be able to fry up some fresh catch for every meal we had, aside from when we would occasionally go to a restaurant.

    I remember how, on this particular day, we were fishing near a bridge that paved the way for traffic and was used regularly. Sometimes you would see people fishing off the side of the bridge. On this day, though, Dad and I were the only ones there. I would normally expect this species to be nocturnal. There was something about the animal that we saw that day that didn't seem to match up with how bright the sun was at that time. Of course, this is just my take, but I do remember my dad also mentioning something along those lines.

So, we were having normal day fishing when suddenly, this entity on two legs came out of the thicket across the river and just stood there looking at us. It didn't make a single noise while it stared at us. It was so creepy because it wouldn't budge from eye contact. I know this sounds dumb, but it felt as if it was engaged in a staring contest with us, an intimidation tactic, I'm sure.

It kind of felt as though this thing hypnotized both my dad and me, but the more I think about it, the more I think that is mostly because we had never seen anything like this entity before. I get what people mean when they say their brains were trying to come off of all sorts of logical answers for something that, at the time, is incomprehensible. It was an awkward feeling staring at something that appears to be out of a storybook.

When I asked Tom if I could submit a report, he asked me to make sure I described the entity to the best of my ability. The river isn't too wide; maybe somewhere around twenty yards. It's been so long since I've been there, that it's hard to give a proper estimate. Anyhow, it wasn't like the entity was right in my face or anything, but I was able to see its entire physique from where I stood. I've heard quite a few people say that the head reminds them of that of a German Shepherd. Even though there were clear differences, I do see what they mean by that statement. Also, I found the colors of its fur to be similar to that of a German Shepherd. But there was something about its face that made me feel like the thing was part human. I can't say why I felt that, but there was just something about its presence that made it seem like *someone* was watching and judging us. It was like it was wondering whether it was worth the hassle to cross the river and kill us or something.

    The entity was tall, definitely much taller than me at the time. I don't think I was even five feet at that age. Before writing this report, I called up my dad to ask him his opinion. He claims that it was definitely over six feet, but he also said it was hunched over, so it was difficult to judge. But, even hunched over, he said the beast was well over six feet. He also agrees that there was something oddly human about the entity—like it was more intelligent than any officially recognized mammal, including apes and dolphins. There was something about its hands that seemed so oddly shaped to me. It was kind of like they were too long and gangly in proportion to the rest of its figure. I see why people refer to it as the "dogman", as there are some similarities. Still, it also has features that I have difficulty relating to anything else that I've ever imagined.

    The entity just kept on staring at us until my dad quietly requested that we gather our stuff and head back to the condo. As you might've suspected, that was the last time we fished at that river. And to tell you the truth, we never did much fishing at all after that. We didn't speak too much about it, but it seemed pretty clear that both of us were too disturbed to spend much time in nature after the strange incident.

I'll admit that seeing that creature has ruined the great outdoors for me. It's not like I haven't gone on outdoor adventures since then; I've gone on many; however, I always have this weird feeling like something is watching me or even stalking me. It's truly amazing how much of an impact these things can make on your brain. For the longest time I didn't want to admit it, but by this point, I'm confident that I suffer from some form of PTSD. And to think... that was only from seeing one of these creatures. I can't even imagine how terrifying it would be to be chased by one.

-Submitted by Jonathan T.

Report #3

For years, I had convinced myself that I had come face-to-face with a real-life werewolf. It wasn't until I started looking into the subject that I came to learn there is a species known as dogmen.

My encounter happened in Featherville, Idaho, in 1978. I had recently graduated high school and had been working as an apprentice for a local carpenter. I was always interested in building stuff, and I knew from a young age that I wanted to work on constructing houses. As a way of furthering my skills on my own time and my own terms, my parents allowed me to renovate a guest house that was in the backyard of a new home that they had recently moved into. I hadn't spent too much time there, but it was truly a beautiful property. The thing must have been over five acres. On the weekends, I would bring over a six-pack of beer and get to work while getting a tan at the same time. It wasn't until the third or fourth weekend that I was working on the guest house when I saw a creature that made me question reality itself. Fortunately, I was up on the roof when I first spotted it.

    I can't say what attracted it to the area, but when my eyes first landed on the figure, it was walking around the guest house on two legs. Honestly, my first reaction was that it was either one of my parents or one of the landscapers that they had come over every few weeks in the spring and summertime. My second thought was that it was someone wearing a quality werewolf mask and wanted to give me a good scare. But I quickly realized that if that were the case, it would have been one of the tallest people I've ever seen in my life. I could tell that even from my perspective up on the roof, the height alone was shocking.

I didn't even say anything when I saw it; I just observed, waiting for it to acknowledge me in some way. I assumed it had to be a person because nothing else made sense at the time. It wasn't even until it wandered off that it dawned on me I might have seen a rare animal. I remember wondering whether it was a bigfoot that I just saw only feet away from me.

Growing up in Idaho, it wasn't all that uncommon to hear rumors about alleged bigfoot sightings, so given the height of this thing, it crossed my mind. I didn't even tell my parents about that first sighting. I was still trying to understand what it was that I had just seen. They were so happy about their new home that I didn't want to risk worrying them. Although I don't think they would've believed me even if I tried to tell them what I saw. They probably would've thought I saw a black bear or large stray dog or whatever. And the worst-case scenario would be that they questioned whether strangers were wandering onto their land.

By the time the following weekend and come around, I had pretty much convinced myself that I had imagined the whole thing. I hadn't told anyone else about it, and I began to doubt the reliability of my memory. Nothing out of the ordinary happened during that next weekend. But it was the weekend after that, where things got even weirder.

I was in the little kitchen area of the guest house, installing a brand-new refrigerator when I noticed movement through the nearest window. When I got closer to the window, I saw the hind legs of something that was bent over and focused on something on the ground in front of it. See, the main reason I thought it was a werewolf was that while I was looking at it through the window, I could've sworn I heard it mumbling something to itself; not anything in

English, or any language I had heard, but it seemed clear that there was form to it. I should mention that that was the only time I thought I heard the thing speak, so I suppose I could've mistaken it for something else. I've never seen any other reports where a dogman allegedly spoke, but given how many reports there are that involve sasquatch, is it that farfetched of an idea?

    I remember how I walked over to the door and locked it before I strolled back over to the window. The creature was still present, so I banged on the wall, hoping to startle it so that it would run back to wherever it came from. Surprised, it leaped backward a few feet, and that's when it locked eyes with me. There was something so sinister about the way it looked at me. I'm convinced that I saw legitimate anger in those eyes.

I got so freaked out when it locked eyes with me, that I walked into the bedroom, closed the curtains, and waited there for I don't know how long. I wanted to call my parents to warn them not to walk over to the guest house, but the telephone line hadn't yet been set up. I kind of just stood there trying to gather my thoughts while listening for any sign that the creature might still be near.

I can't say why I had such a worse feeling compared to the first time I saw the creature, but I guess it had something to do with looking into its eyes. I'm not very religious or anything but when I was looking at it, I got this horrible feeling, like I was looking into the eyes of a demon or something. This thing had no positive energy to it at all; that I can say for sure.

Eventually, I was startled by a knock at the front door and the jiggling of the doorknob. Of course, I wondered whether the creature was trying to make its way inside, and it was creepy as all hell to think that it might know how to use the door handle. It wasn't long before I heard the voice of my dad. He was calling out, asking why I had locked the door, as well as if I wanted an afternoon snack. Worried that he could be out there with the creature, I rushed over to the door, pulled him inside, and once again locked the door behind me.

My dad looked so disturbed, and the very first thing he asked was whether I was on dope. He said I looked all sweaty and like I had been up all night partying or something. After I assured him that wasn't the case, I told him about the creature outside. That was when he revealed to me that he had also seen something that he couldn't identify. He said he saw it climb up a tree, and it was the noise that directed his attention to something that he thought was a hairy human heading up into the tops of the pine trees. Of course, he said that in a way that insinuated that he was mistaken. To him, his eyes had been playing tricks on him, and he thought it had to be an oversized bobcat or something like that. Whatever he thought it was, he wasn't the least bit concerned by it. I thought he was taking it way too lightly. My dad was a strong and confident guy, but I was worried that this was a circumstance where his confidence might get him and Mom injured, if not killed. When I saw that dogman looking at me, there was no question that it could tear all three of us limb from limb. At the time, I couldn't believe that these things were walking around in peoples' backyards, yet nobody is warned about them. The thought of that angered me. As crazy as it sounds, I yearned for a productive way to warn the whole country of what lurks out there. I wanted to explain to people that they should never allow their kids to roam around in or near the woods without close supervision, and even then, it was still incredibly risky.

My dad eventually convinced me that the coast was clear, so I walked with him back to the main house. That short stroll felt so much longer than it was. I kept thinking that the dogman was going to charge out of the woods at any given moment. When we made it inside, my mom quickly asked what was wrong. My dad jumped in explained to her that

I must've glimpsed the "oversized bobcat" and had mistaken it for something else. His tone implied that he didn't want me worrying her. I couldn't blame him for that, yet I also felt a nagging responsibility to be honest so that she'd keep an eye peeled when walking around the property. Because of the timing, it felt like such a predicament. Obviously, I didn't want my parents to regret purchasing the property, but I also didn't want them to get mauled by that freakish looking creature.

Ultimately deciding that it was best to remain composed and show minimal signs of fear, I did all I could to proceed as normal with the renovation. I was pleasantly surprised that my desire to complete the project ended up overpowering my feelings of fear. The weeks carried on normally, and I had begun to wonder if the creature had maybe migrated to another area. Enough time had passed that I even began to question whether I had experienced delusions and that just maybe my dad was correct to say that my perceptions weren't accurate. Fortunately, I had finished the renovation without complication, and I was delighted by how much it seemed to satisfy my parents. They looked forward to providing future guests with a charming and comfortable place to sleep. Soon, my speculation about the strange creature would settle.

It was the weekend when I was over at my parents' house for an early evening barbecue. One of their neighbors, Carol, was over also over. Mom and Dad learned that she had recently lost her husband, and they were trying to show her support and distract her from her sorrow.

I distinctly remember Carol saying, "What is that?" while she stared out the window. The tone of her voice made it obvious that something bizarre had caught her attention. When I turned my attention out the window, that was when all suspicion that I might've been imagining the animal was squashed. There it was, pacing back and forth on two feet, sniffing the air. Right away, I could tell that it had been drawn to the smell of the food that was grilling outside. Luckily, it had been one of those rainy days, causing us to socialize inside whenever the cooking meat didn't need attention. All four of us were inside when the dogman appeared. When it proceeded toward the location of the grill, I was shocked when my dad began heading toward the door to shoo it off. I had to stand in front of the door and convince him to sit down. He was worried that the meat was going to burn if someone didn't remove it from the grill. That was the least of my worries at the time; all I could think about was that the dogman was going to attempt to make its way inside after realizing that the grill was too hot to remove the food. Of course, that was when I assumed that the creature's intelligence was akin to that of the average wolf.

It sent chills up my spine as the four of us stared through the window and watched the creature use one of its large hands to grip the handle and open the grill. Its body language conveyed that it had previously dealt with that kind of contraption on several occasions.

Furthermore, it didn't even attempt to remove the meat with its hands. Even though the tongs were resting on a plate beside the grill, it walked over and grabbed a stick from the nearby ground and used it to nudge the meat off the flames.

After most of the meat fell onto the concrete, the creature got down on both knees and consumed it like a savage. It was at that moment that I felt like I was watching a homeless man with a dog's head eat its first meal of the month. My brain had so much trouble deciding whether I was looking at something that was more man or more animal. As I looked into my dad's eyes, I could tell that he was ready to forfeit any beliefs that we were dealing with something even remotely normal. In fact, he even apologized to me for implying that I was overreacting.

As we continued to watch the animal feed, Carol brought up how she had heard the oddest of noises outside her bedroom window plenty of times. Her deceased husband, George, had grown to believe that it was some kind of extraterrestrial activity because they both agreed they could hear the dialogue, but it sounded completely foreign to them. Every time George went to go peek out the window, he never had luck spotting anything.

Though she never outright said it, it seemed that Carol thought this dogman was of extraterrestrial origin, and I can't lie; I sometimes wonder if that could be the case. It's just so suspicious to me that these creatures can exist, yet they're not officially documented by science. Like, what the hell could be the reason for that? The theory that I find most believable is that creatures like dogman and sasquatch lead to other even more disturbing truths—truths that the government has deemed too disruptive for society to learn. It makes you think about who or what is watching us from the shadows at all times, all while we're usually without the slightest clue.

As you likely expected, the dogman was efficient at devouring the meat, and once it was finished, it ran on all fours around the house and out of sight. That was the first time I had seen it move on all fours. Up until that point, I assumed it walked upright at all times. I guess they are similar to the sasquatch species in that they are efficient at both stances.

When we eventually went outside later that evening to switch the grill off, my dad and I noticed quite a few drops of blood around the area of the grill. Normally, we would've ruled that the blood came from the meat; however, it was too well done by the time the creature slid it off the grill.

Neither my parents nor I ever saw the dogman again after that, but we did end up moving down to Arizona about a year later. Since we never saw the dogman again, we often speculated if the blood could've been a sign that the rare animal was badly wounded. If that was the case, had it been injured by gunfire? Or maybe it had a violent encounter with another one of its kind or even a sasquatch. I guess some things will forever remain secret. I encourage you to have someone else with you when you venture out into nature, or at the very least, carry a sturdy weapon to defend yourself.

-Submitted by anonymous

Report #4

I want to start by saying how relieved I am that the dogman is finally getting some much-needed attention. It is a very real species, and I've been made to feel crazy by so many of my peers ever since I had my encounter nearly 25 years ago.

My name is Sally, and I ran into the rare predator back when I lived in Cody, Wyoming. I wouldn't say I grew up there, but I spent a significant amount of time there and always felt that I was surrounded by good energy until that very day.

When I was in my mid-twenties, I used to be a guide for a little horseback riding operation that was really close to Yellowstone National Park. Because of its proximity to the park, we were usually pretty busy with tourists, aside from the winter months. I did it for close to four years, and almost every day was the same routine. Because of the location, you would expect that we saw a lot more wildlife than we did. I noticed that animals in and around Yellowstone National Park are pretty efficient when it comes to avoiding people. Plus, you have to remember that so many people that go there bring children along. Those children usually don't understand that laughing and screaming more often than not deters the animals that so many of them hope to see. However, this wasn't one of those cases; in actuality, I think the noisy children had attracted the rare beast.

I remember it was a crisp fall day, and the leaves were as colorful as ever. The air was extremely brisk because the family had scheduled a ride for 6:00 AM. The two kids—one girl and one boy—complained about how early they had to wake up. Apparently, they had a very eventful day ahead and needed to do the earliest ride possible so that it wouldn't conflict with anything else. That was fine with me; I've always been an early riser, as I learned early in life that I'm less irritable when I feel I'm always on the go.

As how kids often are, they eventually gathered enough energy and became rather hyper. We often had to ask the children to calm down because the horses clearly didn't appreciate it when they were overly loud. I've never much believed in it, but maybe it's true that some kids really do have that ADD or ADHD or whatever.

We were on what was the most popular of the four trails and been at it for an hour or so when I suddenly noticed something totally scary off to my left. In the thicket, was this hunched-over creature that appeared to be flanking us. I don't get how it's possible, but the thing seriously moved with total silence. Its motion made it look like it was quickly tiptoeing alongside us. At first, I thought it was a large naked man, but then I quickly noticed it was covered in dark brown fur and had what looked like the head of a coyote. It was seriously so weird looking that my jaw must've been hanging from my mouth. I'm surprised nobody noticed that I was acting funny right then and there. Perhaps the most disturbing part about the sighting was the fact that it was staring directly at the children. It was easy to see that it was perfectly aligned with them; its gaze locked onto the boy—who I should mention was the younger of the kids. Even though he was sitting on the saddle in front of his mom, I could tell that the animal was licking its lips, likely hoping we'd take a break at some point and leave it with a better opportunity to snag its prey.

    I didn't want to say anything because my instinct told me that if I pointed out the creature, everyone would begin to panic and, thus, enter fight or flight mode. I had never seen a creature like that before, but I already saw enough to know that it was an apex predator, and I didn't want to do anything that would provoke it to charge us. The thing was so large that there was no question whether it would be able to tip a horse with minimal effort. All it would have to do was to pounce on the horse, and the parents and child would come tumbling down with it. I was never even the slightest bit tempted to shout at it with the hope that it might run off; it was obvious that that would lead to an unwanted result. I remember being rather surprised that none of our horses seemed to pick up on the fact that there was a predator around the size of a grizzly bear stalking us, and who knows how long it was before I spotted it.

Since we were over the halfway point through the trail, I thought the best possible thing I could do in that situation was to keep quiet, pretend like I hadn't seen anything, and hope that we made it back to the ranch before the creature decided to attack. I figured that the closer we got to civilization, the better our chances were that the creature would stop following us any further.

I was trying so hard to remain calm and cool, but I'm sure the family had suddenly felt as if I was stoic and uptight. It's so incredibly tough to hide it when you're terrified out of your mind. Since I was in front of everyone, I made sure to limit the number of times I looked to my left, because I didn't want the others to notice any one thing had captured my attention. I'd say it was a good 100 feet away from us or so, and it blended in so well with the environment, that it helped it to go undetected. The whole time I was bracing myself for any of them to start screaming after noticing it for themselves. I felt as if I was near a ticking timebomb, but without knowing how much time was left before the explosion.

Luckily, the particular horses that we had were very tame and weren't easily spooked like so many others. I always made fun of them for being a lot more like donkeys than horses. They were all on the shorter and fatter side, and sort of oblivious to a lot that was going on around them; fortunately, that helped to keep things calm.

I kid you not; it was the entire time since I first noticed the creature, that it kept its eyes locked on the small boy. It was when were about five minutes away from the ranch that it veered out of my sight. It didn't return after that.

For what I believe to be obvious reasons, I never told the tourist family what had stalked us that day. I think that could've only led to negative consequences; either they'd get freaked out that a monster was in the area, likely warn others to avoid our business, or they'd look at me like I'm crazy... and then warn others to avoid our business. I did tell the owner of the business because she knew me well enough to know that I'm not one to make stuff up or exaggerate. And that was when she revealed to me that she thought she had seen a sasquatch on a couple of occasions, once while she was standing in her driveway, and another time while she was on a road trip a few hours from the town of Cody. I've begun to realize that these encounters are nowhere near as rare as I once thought. I'd be willing to bet that they occur somewhere in North America every day.

I can't help but wonder if the sasquatch species and dogman species are at all associated; my boss's stories wouldn't be the only time that I heard about them coexisting in the same territory. I've lived around the wilderness, but I haven't seen anything else like the dogman since that day. I've heard many strange sounds, but the reality is that regularly documented animals are capable of making such a wide array of noises. All you have to do is spend a single night camping in the woods to understand what I'm talking about.

-Submitted by Sally F.

Are you enjoying the read?

Due to the unexpected success of my books, I have decided to give back to the readers by making the following eBook **FREE** for anyone who wants it!

To claim your free eBook, head over to

www.LivingAmongBigfoot.com

and click the "FREE BOOK" tab!

Report #5

I haven't seen the dogman myself, but my grandfather used to talk about it all the time, which led to my interest in the topic. He lived in a very small town in Indiana, known as Batesville. I just checked while I'm writing this, and the current population is right around 6,400. I haven't been back to that town since Grandpa Eric passed away twelve years ago, but he had quite a few acres to himself.

I'm not overplaying how relevant the dogman was to Grandpa Eric; he even always said that his obsession with the rare creature was the main reason my grandmother divorced him and moved to the Chicago area to be closer to her sister. My grandpa was a tax accountant for the majority of his life, and according to him, it was while he was on his way to the office one day that he saw a dogman cross the road. He always described it as being by far the largest animal he'd ever seen. He referred to it as 'the wolfman' until he read some book that mentioned dogmen are a legitimate species that merely has yet to be publicized by mainstream science.

According to Grandpa Eric, the dogman jumped in front of his car, causing him to slam on the brakes, and then it ran alongside the road before jumping back onto the street, causing the only other car on the road to swerve into the grass. Understandably, neither he nor the other driver was brave enough to step out of their vehicles, and the other person drove off before Grandpa Eric could confirm what they had just witnessed.

When I was a child, that story always thrilled me. As I grew older, I started to wonder how much truth there was to his stories. I wondered how much they could have been embellished. But over the last five years, I've read all sorts of books and have watched many videos on YouTube, and it's no secret that people all over the world experience events that are just as alarming, if not more. Doing that helped me to realize that Grandpa Eric's encounters were just a few of millions.

I remember him going as far as to say that he was grateful to the dogman for exposing itself to him because his life had become so mundane before that. Even though that first sighting shook him to his core, he stated that it added mystery and intrigue to his existence. At the risk of sounding comical, I suppose you could say he had become somewhat of a dogman detective.

I don't know how long it was after he had that initial sighting, but he returned to the scene at a time when traffic would be minimal. He always said he got the impression that the creature was trying to intimidate him and the other driver and steer them out of the area. He thought that maybe it was guarding something. His hunch might've been correct, as he discovered a large skeleton that only could've belonged to a cow. It was about 80% consumed and was cleverly hidden within a ditch that was between a barbed fence and some bushes. As he glanced around the area, he spotted cows way off in the distance on the other side of that fence. That disturbed Grandpa Eric, because it likely meant that the dogman tossed the body of the adult-sized cow over the fence.

Keep in mind that the average weight of a fully-grown cow is 1500 lbs. The possibility that anyone or anything could've lifted something that heavy off the ground and avoided injury is staggering. Grandpa also claimed that there were enormous droppings nearby the carcass. That further affirmed to him that the creature might be dwelling in that area. Suddenly, he got the idea that it wasn't too wise to be sticking around there without any means of protection. He did talk about how an intense feeling of fear washed over him at that moment. I think these cryptids are extremely interesting, but I would've hightailed it out of there long before he got that bad feeling.

Because he was in such a small town, it wasn't long before he started telling locals about what he had encountered, especially amid throwing back a few cold ones at the local watering hole. I don't think it was to anyone's surprise when people began to mock him. I'm sure that even he expected that to happen. Still, his obsession continued, and he would frequently drive all over the country roads, keeping an eye out for anything strange. Because of his interest in the subject matter, he was staying out more and more and spending less time with my grandma. She didn't like how everyone would ask her about how her husband's "werewolf investigations" were going. Apparently, she never believed that whatever he saw was a cryptid; she insisted that it must have been an oversized, stray mongrel. Eventually, that led to a lot of conflict between my grandparents; thus, they ended up separating and remained that way.

There's no doubt that my grandfather went through some hard times. His wife had left him, and he was so fixated on proving to everyone who knew him that he hadn't imagined the creature. One night he pulled over on the side of the road after having had a little too much liquor, and one of the local police officers walked up to the driver's side door and woke him up to make sure that he was alright. Since my grandfather was extremely drunk, he had expected to get arrested. Instead, the younger police officer revealed to him that he, too, had seen the dogman. That was the first time that anyone had openly admitted to him that he wasn't alone on the subject matter. Even though my grandpa knew he wasn't crazy, this knowledge helped him to feel more at ease.

Allegedly, the young police officer had responded to an emergency call that happened near the edge of town. It was an older woman who claimed that a wolfman had eaten her pitbull. Though he didn't believe some of the specifics of her story at first, he was very startled when he checked out the remains of the pitbull. He said that little more than a skeleton remained and that he was amazed how quickly the mystery predator stripped the poor pet of its flesh. He said that it was while he was shining the flashlight on the skeleton that the predator came charging out of the woods and forced him back inside. Together, he and the homeowner watched the large dogman as it proceeded to gnaw on the remains, often splitting various bones as though they were nothing thicker than toothpicks.

It's probably Needless to say that the officer called for backup, but even though they responded quickly, it was too late; the dog man had carried the remaining bones into the meadow that surrounded the property, never to return that night. He received news that the homeowner died not too long after that, so he couldn't be sure whether the ferocious predator still lingered in the vicinity.

The officer didn't provide the exact address, but my grandpa remembered that an old widow had recently died, and he knew that dense meadow surrounded her house. He thanked the officer for being so kind and understanding, and he headed for home.

I believe it was the following day that he went to go check out the property that he suspected the officer referred to. Since nobody seemed to have purchased the place, he had no trouble walking into the backyard and taking a glimpse at the meadow. That's how ballsy of a guy my grandfather was. If he wanted something, he'd go after it.

If there were consequences to his actions, he was willing to take them on. Having no complications the first time around, he ended up visiting that property multiple times, and even brought a polaroid camera, hoping to finally obtain a bit of proof.

According to my grandfather, he spotted the dogman during his fourth visit when he went there at dusk. He claimed that he saw its head poking out of the meadow. Since nobody seemed to be occupying the house, his theory was that the creature had been sleeping in the meadow. He said it was so high and dense that it would've been the best location in the area to hide. It would've provided enough cover, while also allowing easy access to prey like rabbits and deer.

He snapped a few shots with his polaroid camera; apparently, the creature acted intrigued every time the shutter sounded off. There was something about its body language at that moment that made him feel more at ease; the creature didn't seem at all interested in pursuing him. Grandpa would joke about how it must've recently fed, thus causing it to essentially dismiss his presence. He guessed that the creature was about 80 yards out in the meadow but that its height eliminated the possibility that it could be anything else. I want to mention that I've read Tom's book, *Stranger from the Meadow*, and it fascinated me that both the sasquatch species and dogman species could utilize some of the same strategies.

My grandpa claimed that there was always a very ominous feeling when he was near this creature's territory. He strongly believed that it was the same creature that he saw on both occasions. Also, although he believed to have had only seen one of them, he often talked about how there must be more of them in the area. He thought the idea that there could be only one Bigfoot, Lochness Monster, Yeti, etc. was absurd, and it was no different regarding the dogman. To him, no creature would remain in a location that didn't present an opportunity to reproduce; that would go against nature in every way.

The photographs turned out surprisingly good... at least, in my opinion. But when my grandpa would show them to locals, they tended to brush him off; not a single person, aside from the friendly police officer took them at all seriously. Since they're polaroids, they heavily faded over time, but they were still in good enough quality to make out a tall figure standing in the middle of the meadow. I thought about submitting them to this publication, but I was worried that people would just accuse them of being staged. It's interesting how so many people seem so willing to hear about encounters of this nature, but once you claim to have photographic evidence, the naysayers come after you.

There is one more encounter story that my grandfather told me about, but I thought it might be better to save it for another issue of *Dogman Frightening Encounters*. Maybe Tom will be able to persuade me to share the photographs. If you've had encounters with the sasquatch or dogman species, I highly recommend you shoot Tom a message; he loves to discuss your experiences and is one of the nicest dudes involved in the bigfoot community!

-Submitted by Ryan H.

Report #6

It's so interesting to me how we grow up being told by our parents that monsters are not real. If you're reading this report, along with the rest of this book, chances are you know that monsters are indeed very real. Sure, you could say that the dogman is just another species of animal, but at what point do we begin to separate animals from monsters? Also, are we told that they're not real so that society can function without minimal fear daily? I believe that authority figures don't see it as productive for the rhythm of society, probably for multiple reasons.

My name is Sam, and my encounter happened just last year in dripping Springs, Texas. My cousin, Rob, and I were swimming in this really cool pond that feels much more like an enchanted lagoon. The place is known as Hamilton pool preserve, and it is most certainly the small town's claim to fame. It gives the location a lot of charm that it wouldn't have otherwise. The more I think about it, the more I realize it was the perfect setting to cross paths with a real-life monster. Both Rob and I are in our late-20s, and it's not at all uncommon for us to finish off a case of beer by ourselves. Over the last six years, we have been passionate about exercising and trying to be as strong as possible. I suppose you could say it was a very healthy rivalry between the two of us, as we both have similar builds and levels of strength. I bring this up because we've convinced ourselves that excessive beer drinking helps us to be stronger than we would be otherwise. We're not intimidated by very much, but this was a situation where I'm surprised that neither of us crapped our swimsuits.

We hadn't been at the Hamilton pool preserve for very long, only having had two or three beers, when suddenly, we heard some extremely loud commotion emanating from the woods around us. It sounded like two large animals fighting for some unknown reason. There exists a variety of wildlife in that area, but I had never heard anything close to that noise. It was like something out of a science-fiction movie. I've said to many people that it sounded like a scene in the film, *Jurassic Park*. If you've seen the movie and remember what the velociraptors sounded like when they were feasting on the cow, that truly is the closest thing I can relate it to. Anyway, the commotion silenced us, and we waited for a few minutes, wondering if we were going to get a visual of what was happening. I can remember how we Kept glancing at one another, waiting for the other person to develop an explanation for whatever the hell these things were.

Finally, this surprisingly large animal darted out of the woods and came very close to the shore that was on the opposite end of where we were standing in the knee-high water. Even though it was a good distance away, we still had a good visual of the creature. What was interesting was how it never once turned to look at us; it was far more concerned with whatever it had been tangling with in the woods. Its rapid breathing gave me the impression that it was extremely exhausted from whatever it was fighting with. Rob and I were the only ones there at the time, and I always wished that there was at least one other person there to discuss what we saw. What's weird was how it was probably the only time we had ever been there by ourselves. The location is popular amongst the small town, so it's difficult to get it to yourself. So, it was a rare occasion in a variety of ways.

When the creature first emerged from the woods, I thought I was looking at a devil in physical form. There was something about the shape of the legs that brought about that idea. But I soon saw the pointed ears and the long snout and realized that I was looking at something of dog origin. It reminded me of the hieroglyphics that you see in Egypt; The ones that illustrate the gods as having a head more like that of a dog's.

Although I could make out a lot of the detail on this creature, it was still too far away to judge its size accurately. But whenever I've been asked to guesstimate, I say that it was probably a little bit larger than the two of us. It paced along the shore for under a minute before dashing back into the woods. Of course, I can't say for sure, but it looked like it was prepared to head back into battle. Rob and I continue to stand there watching, waiting for additional aggressive noises, but nothing further came about. Maybe whatever the creature was fighting with decided to move along before it in endured further damage.

I've been back to location multiple times since that day, and I've never seen or heard anything like it. I am convinced that I've seen a UFO, but that's an entirely different story for another time. Having had both of those experiences, I now can't help but laugh at anyone who says these kinds of things are mythical. It just goes to show how naïve so many people, especially in this country, truly are. But it's not even their fault. They only know what generations before them have told them. I'm grateful for people like Tom Lyons, people who aren't afraid to share their experiences that so many people will view as too ridiculous to have taken place. I've noticed that it even takes a good amount of courage to convince yourself of these bizarre events. Society has done a fine job at programming too many of us to remain quiet out of fear of being mocked.

The way I see it is that, if you contribute your report to the public eye, you are doing a good deed because it encourages more people to be brave and share their own experiences. Some will disagree, but I believe that the more often we distribute these reports, the harder it is for authority figures to continue the suppression. We were put on this earth just like anyone else; therefore, we deserve to know the truth about what's out there. I don't think anyone should have the right to withhold that kind of information from anyone; it's just not right. Anyhow, I will leave it at that. I appreciate the invitation to send you my report, Tom.

-Submitted by Samuel G.

Report #7

Hello there, my name is Melissa and, and I thought for the longest time that I had encountered an oversized baboon. It was years later that I learned about the mysterious dogman species. There is something so deeply ominous about them. I've read that sasquatch presents comparable energy, but I have never seen one, so I'm not able to compare.

I am now 59 years young, and my experience occurred back in 1986, in Oshkosh, Wisconsin. Oddly enough, it happened less than a week before Halloween of that year, so naturally, some tried to convince me that I saw someone in a werewolf costume. I suppose that would be possible for someone who suffers from drug-induced hallucinations, but I've been sober almost my entire life. I've never been into experimenting with substances and have always had a crystal-clear mind. Sure, I sip on wine every once in a while, but Intelligent people know that that cannot trigger hallucinations.

I had recently broken up with a boy that I was very in love with and needed some time to myself to embrace my emotions. I had been walking around in nature almost every day during the month that it happened, and it was when I was at a nearby forest preserve that I stumbled upon the rare animal. It was while I was walking uphill, and I spotted the animal sitting on top of a large boulder. Something that has always amazed me is how it was clear that I was aware of it before it was aware of me. I know this because I'll never forget how it's head perked up and its eyes widened as it heard me semi-slip on a few pebbles.

I then watched as its mouth slowly opened and formed what looked to me like a menacing smile. The smile was a lot like how the Joker smiles, only add sharp teeth. There was something about the way it looked at me that made me believe I was moments away from getting torn to pieces. Truthfully, I remember not caring very much. I was so depressed from my breakup that I think I would have been all right dying at that moment. I think that is the only reason I didn't immediately turn and run in the opposite direction.

Its fur was a very dark brown color and had a tint of gold. However, the gold tint could've been caused by the bits of sunlight that pierced through the trees. Its ears and snout were black. I've read all the reports that describe the shape of the head to be a lot like a coyote's, but I thought it looked a lot more like a baboon's. I think that one of the other reasons I thought it was an ape of some kind was because I could make out sets of hands and feet, as opposed to paws and claws. I once told one of my friends who has native American roots, and it was his opinion that what I saw was a skinwalker. Honestly, I prefer to not think of it that way, because that seems so much creepier than a dogman. When I think of skinwalkers, I think of witchcraft and magic and all that other stuff, and it makes me feel as though whatever I encountered could still be haunting me.

Another creepy aspect of this sighting was the position in which the creature was sitting. Its posture reminded me of how you'll often see children sit—with their knees just below their chin. I can't say exactly why I feel this way, but I'm confident that it was an adult. It slowly rose to its feet, and I noticed how the feet were quite long and curved around the boulder, similar to what monkeys can do with their feet; it definitely had an extremely strong grip.

It stood up for somewhere between five and ten seconds before transitioning to a crouching position. Its legs looked so powerful that I felt it could've leaped all the way over to me with minimal effort. Although it was insanely muscular everywhere, I couldn't help but notice that its belly was protruding. It didn't match the rest of its build, so I think that it had only just finished a large meal. Maybe that was what prevented it from attacking me because it soon climbed down the other side of the boulder, and I never saw it again. Suddenly, my wits kicked in and told me to head back to my car. Luckily, it wasn't even a mile away in reality, but it felt so much further because I was so afraid.

    I was living with my mom and stepdad back then, and I told them about the encounter as soon as I saw them later that day. Surprisingly, they seemed to believe me. I don't know if it was because they were trying to be agreeable, given what I was going through, but they both were very open about my interpretation of what I saw. It was very comforting, and that's something I've always appreciated when I looked back on it. It's a shame that not everyone who encounters cryptids has someone who will trust them on the matter, or at least be willing to listen with open ears.

In a sense, I felt that that frightening encounter was a blessing in disguise; it was sufficient at distracting me from the grief I was feeling, and it expanded my world view. I always had this inkling that we were being lied to on multiple fronts, and it was nice to confirm that I wasn't a fool for having thought such things.

My daughter was the first to introduce me to the works of Tom Lyons after she came across his Instagram account. She convinced me to create my own account so that I could stay in the loop, and it was as soon as I discovered he had released the first volume of *Dogman Frightening Encounters* that I knew I had to participate.

Thank you, Tom, for your willingness to review my report!

-Submitted by Melissa F.

Report #8

If you've ever been to Marietta, Ohio, perhaps you'd agree that it has a charming but ghostly feel to it. My encounter with a dogman happened while I was visiting my college girlfriend back in 2006. We're both from Ohio and met while studying at the great Ohio State University.

My girlfriend, who I'll give the name Lauren, knew that I was obsessed with all outdoor activities, so she surprised me with a kayaking trip that was meant to last a few hours. The day got off to a great start; things like kayaking always got me into my best possible mood. It was amazing how quickly things could turn dark.

I don't think we had even been kayaking for an hour when suddenly, we spotted a man in uniform who was standing alongside the river and awaiting us to get closer so that he could speak to us. He waved us down, so it was immediately evident that whatever he had to say was important. By the time we have paddled close enough to him, I could see around the band that there were armed professionals. At first, it looked to me like the SWAT team had been called over to respond to an emergency of some kind. As I continued to observe the man, I soon realized that they were not police officers, but rather military personnel.

I was so distracted by the activity that I only gathered bits and pieces of what the forest ranger was saying to us. He said that he would call for someone with a trailer to pick us and the kayaks up since he wasn't legally allowed us to go any further. He also made it very clear that he wasn't permitted to reveal any of the details to us.

It was while Lauren and I had begun to drag the kayaks out of the water, that we heard the hair-raising growl, followed by gunfire. The only thing that I could assume at the time was that the men had been summoned to track down an aggressive mountain lion or black bear. However, my assumption that they were dealing with an ordinary animal would soon be put to rest. Out of nowhere, an extremely tall and hairy figure came running around the riverbank and was hobbling straight toward where we were standing. When looking back on it, something that is a tad humorous, was how the ranger ran into the water before instructing us on what to do. Naturally, we did the same as him, fully immersing ourselves into the cool water.

Although the dogman eyed us as it hobbled onward, it was as if it knew it had no time for us. Of course, I'm so grateful for that because that thing was fully capable of being a killing machine. I can't imagine any living thing standing a chance at surviving if this creature designated it as prey. I've heard some people say that a bigfoot might be able to hold its own against one of these things, but I've never seen one, so it's hard to imagine anything giving the dogman a run for its money.

Tom asked me to provide a detailed description of what the creature looked like, and I think the best way of doing that would be to tell you to go online and look up the lycans from the *Underworld* film series. This thing was just as muscular as those creatures, if not more so. I'm also going to go ahead and say I believe it was taller than any of the creatures in those movies. I hope that whatever I saw was a full-grown adult because if not, the idea that any land predator could grow larger chills me to my core. I feel like something of that size could take down an African elephant single-handedly.

I believe that the only reason the creature didn't kill every single one of those military men was that it was likely drugged up. I could tell by its body language that this was no unintelligent organism. It wasn't long before the man came around the corner and started firing at the creature. There was no question that they wanted to prevent any more civilians from seeing the thing. I'm not sure whether any bullets penetrated the creature, since it continued to hobble at high speed in the other direction. Just after the creature disappeared from our sights, a black helicopter entered the area and hovered above the nearby woods that the creature had likely entered.

Even though the ranger seemed to be almost as shocked by all of this as we were, he warned us that we were going to need to sign confidentiality agreement forms before we'd be permitted to leave the area. He was right; before the van came to pick us up along with the kayaks, a man in military fatigue brought out a binder from their vehicle that contained a stack of paper. It was a black binder that looked like it had been around for quite some time. I couldn't help but wonder how many signatures it had inside of it. Was this ordeal more of a common thing than I would've thought?

It all happened so fast that it's hard to give it some storybook ending. They had all of our information, and we were expected to remain quiet about it. Lauren is now my wife, and we have told various close friends throughout the years, at least the ones who we suspected would be interested, but I get the feeling that few of them believe us. I think they believe that something out of the ordinary happened, but it was likely a bear that we had mistaken for some mythical beast.

Just as with so many other reports I've read, the experience gave birth to a new hobby for both Lauren and I. We've calmed down a little bit since then, but there was a time when we were reading, listening to, and watching every piece of dogman related content we could get our hands on. When you realize there is so much more to this existence than you had originally thought, it tends to make life more interesting than it was; at least, that's how it was for Lauren and I. However, I can imagine it being suffocating if you're the only one out of everyone you know who has had encounters with cryptids.

There's no question that it was therapeutic for both her and I to have someone so close to review the event with. I do believe that the whole thing brought us closer, and you wouldn't believe how deep some of the discussions get between us. It feels like we are immersed in this ongoing mystery that will likely never get solved.

-Submitted by anonymous

Are you interested in Tom's experience with the sasquatch species?

The popular "Living Among Bigfoot" series is now available on Amazon, Audible, and iTunes!

Editor's Note

Before you go, I'd very much like to say "thank you" for purchasing this book.

I'm aware you had an endless variety of bigfoot-related books to choose from, but you took a chance on my content. Therefore, thanks for reading this one and sticking with it to the last page.

At this point, I'd like to ask you for a *tiny* favor; it would mean the world to me if you could leave a review on this book's Amazon.com page.

Your feedback will aid me as I continue to create products that you, as well as others, can enjoy.

Mailing List Sign Up Form

Don't forget to sign up for the newsletter email list. I promise this will not be used to spam you, but only to ensure that you will always receive the first word on any new releases, discounts, or giveaways! All you need to do is visit the following URL and enter your email address.

URL-

http://eepurl.com/dhnspT

Social Media

Feel free to follow/reach out to me with any questions or concerns on either Instagram or Twitter! I will do my best to follow back and respond to all comments.

Instagram:
@living_among_bigfoot

Twitter:
@AmongBigfoot

About the Editor

A simple man at heart, Tom Lyons lived an ordinary existence for his first 52 years. Native to the great state of Wisconsin, he went through the motions of everyday life, residing near his family and developing a successful online business. The world that he once knew would completely change shortly after moving out west, where he was confronted by the allegedly mythical species known as Bigfoot.

You can email him directly at:

Living.Among.Bigfoot@gmail.com

Also, check out Tom Lyon's author page on Amazon:

https://amzn.to/2PRTyOw

Made in the USA
Middletown, DE
17 January 2022